DUELISTS, START YO
5D's
YU-GI-OH!
Story by Masahiro Hikokubo
Art by Masashi Sato
Production Support: STUDIO DICE
A high speed Turbo Duel through the streets of Satellite brings Yusei Fudo and his friend Sect face to face with an urban legend incarnate! Will Yusei lose Sect to the Skeleton Knight? And what sinister plans does Jack Atlas, master of New Domino City have in store for Yusei?
Available Now from
VIZ Media
ISBN: 978-1-4215-3963-8
PRICE: $9.99 US/ $12.99 CAN
MORE FROM THE WORLD OF YU-GI-OH!
VISIT WWW.VIZ.COM FOR THE ENTIRE LIBRARY OF YU-GI-OH! MANGA
Available at your local bookstore or comic store
YU-GI-OH! 5D's © 2009 by Masahiro Hikokubo, Masashi Sato/SHUEISHA Inc.
© K. Takahashi
© NAS • TV TOKYO
YU-GI-OH! GX © 2005 by Kazuki Takahashi, Naoyuki Kageyama/SHUEISHA Inc.
© K. Takahashi
© NAS/TV TOKYO
YU-GI-OH! R © 2004 by Kazuki Takahashi, Akira Ito/SHUEISHA Inc.
SHONEN JUMP MANGA
www.shonenjump.com
RATED T FOR TEEN
ratings.viz.com
viz media
www.viz.com

SHONEN JUMP
DEATH NOTE
デスノート
"The human whose name is written in this note shall die."
DEATH NOTE
Black Edition
I
Story by: Tsugumi Ohba
Art by: Takeshi Obata
KILLER 2-IN-1 VALUE AND EXCLUSIVE COLOR PAGES
ISBN 13: 978-1-4215-3964-5
$ 14.99 USA | $ 16.99 CAN
INCLUDES THE ENTIRE MANGA SERIES, DEATH NOTE HOW TO READ 13 AND HOW TO USE DEATH NOTE BOOKLET
ISBN 13: 978-1-4215-2581-5
$ 99.99 USA | $ 109.99 CAN
OWN THE ANIME DVD VOL. 1-9 NOW AVAILABLE
VOL. 1 ISBN 13: 978-1-4215-1853-4
$ 24.92 USA | $ 34.99 CAN
SHONEN JUMP
www.shonenjump.viz.com
deathnote.viz.com
AVAILABLE NOW AT
store.viz.com
AND AT YOUR LOCAL COMIC OR BOOK STORE
RATED T+ FOR OLDER TEEN
ratings.viz.com
DEATH NOTE © 2003 by Tsugumi Ohba, Takeshi Obata/SHUEISHA Inc. DEATH NOTE HOW TO READ 13 © 2006 by Tsugumi Ohba, Takeshi Obata/SHUEISHA Inc.
© Tsugumi Ohba, Takeshi Obata / SHUEISHA, VAP, MAD HOUSE, DNDP All Rights Reserved.

PHONE IN AND THEN...
...FIGHT TO GET OUT!
From the pages of SHONEN JUMP Magazine!
PSYREN
Story and Art by Toshiaki Iwashiro
Ageha Yoshina just got transported to a warped alternate dimension where you've got to fight your way back to our world—or die trying.
PSYREN
1
Story and Art by Toshiaki Iwashiro
ISBN-13- 978-1-4215-3676-7
$9.99 US | $12.99 CAN
SHONEN JUMP
MANGA
www.shonenjump.com
On sale now at
www.viz.com
Also available at your local bookstore or comic store.
PSYREN © 2007 by Toshiaki Iwashiro/SHUEISHA Inc.
RATED T FOR TEEN
ratings.viz.com
VIZ media
www.viz.com

SJ ADVANCED
Can teenage exorcist Allen Walker defeat the Millennium Earl...and save the world?
Manga on sale now!
D.Gray-man
SHONEN JUMP ADVANCED
Story & Art by
KATSURA HOSHINO
D.GRAY-MAN
Katsura Hoshino
D.Gray-man™
$7.99
SHONEN JUMP ADVANCED
D.GRAY-MAN © 2004 by Katsura Hoshino/SHUEISHA Inc.
On sale at:
www.shonenjump.com
Also available at your local bookstore and comic store.
RATED T+ FOR OLDER TEEN
ratings.viz.com
VIZ media
www.viz.co

IN THE NEXT VOLUME...

KYOTO IN DARKNESS

Yokai continue to break the eight seals of Hidemoto, which keep their leader, the dark Hagoromo-Gitsune, bound and powerless. In Kyoto, the scene of the main battle, Rikuo's friend Yura and her allies face one of their own comrades, who is now possessed by an age-old yokai. Meanwhile Rikuo and his fellow Nura clansmen are speeding toward Kyoto via flying boat. But the followers of Hagoromo-Gitsune are determined to make sure their journey is anything but smooth sailing.

AVAILABLE AUGUST 2012!

SHFF...
EH?! What is this, Kana?
If you move, it's going to fall off!
Okay, I'm going home now.
Don't look, and don't touch it--!!
Just stay like that for a while, alright?
I see...it's Valentine's Day...
...so this must be chocolate.
THAT'S...
...NOT GOOD!
...Why?

MNCH
MNCH
MNCH
MNCH

PART 3

HI, NATSUMI!
WHO ARE YOU GOING TO GIVE CHOCOLATE TO?
UM...
TODAY IS VALENTINE'S DAY.
WILL ANYONE GIVE ME CHOCOLATE?
OH...
IS THAT ...
CH-CHOCOLATE? SURELY NOT FOR ME ?!
WE MET HERE, SO I HOPE HE'LL SHOW UP.
I OWE HIM MY LIFE!
THE MONK WITH THE UMBRELLA HAT!!
I doubt he will...
IT WASN'T ...
...ME.
SENBA, I'VE GOT SOME FOR YOU TOO!
DOUBT HE WANTS ANY.
GASP
THE END

VALENTINE'S DAY TRUE STORY PART 2

Volume 9: Tono Monogatari (End)

NO WORRIES!
NURA WILL CATCH UP LATER!!
YAY
YAY
YOU THINK SO?
ANYWAY, WHY ARE WE STARTING AT NIGHT?
BING
IENAGA!! WE'RE ON A YOKAI TOUR!!
WE HAVE TO SEARCH WHILE THE TEMPLES AND SHRINES ARE CLOSED!!
GWOOO
I KNEW I SHOULDN'T HAVE COME...
LOOK!! A YOKAI AURA IS EVERYWHERE!!
I STUDIED ALL ABOUT KYOTO!! RECORDS STATE THAT 234 PEOPLE JUMPED OFF THE STAGE AT KIYOMIZU DURING THE EDO PERIOD!!
ABOUT 85% SURVIVED !!
YIPEE
YIPEE
OH...
IT SURE IS COLD FOR SUMMER ...
TRMBL
...
HM...?
FSSHH

(MAIKO: GEISHA IN TRAINING)

FFSH
THIS IS THE NURA CLAN'S FAMOUS STRATEGIC YOKAI AIRBASE, THE TREASURE SHIP!!!
With suckerhouseboats!!
FFSHU
FFSH
FOR YEARS, IT HAS BEEN AN ABSOLUTE NECESSITY FOR EXCURSIONS!
RIKUO, KYOTO LOOKS GREAT...
...FROM ABOVE!!
DADOOM
WHOA...
NOW THAT'S THE NURA CLAN FOR YOU!
THEY'RE NOT IN DECLINE AT ALL!
GRAMPS...
I never knew about this!

FSSHH
FFSSHH
FFSS
W...
WHAT'S THAT?!
FFSSH

WHAM
WAIT!!
?!
GRAMPS ...?
MUR MUR
YOU SPOILED OUR DRAMATIC DEPARTURE!
LET ME SHOW YOU SOMETHING YOU'LL LIKE.
IT CAME AS SOON AS I CALLED.
GRIN
JAB JAB
RRM
HMM ...
MMRR
... MMMMM ?!
FFSSHH
奴良組
奴良組

READ THIS WAY

GO END THIS.
WHEN YOU RETURN, YOU WILL BE THE THIRD SUPREME COMMANDER.
OH, RIGHT.
WHEN YOU GET TO KYOTO, YOU SHOULD MEET HIDEMOTO.
WHO'S THAT?
ASK AN ONMYOJI GIRL.
...
PREPARE A CELEBRATORY FEAST FOR MY RETURN.

AHH...
VERY GOOD.
WELL, DO AS YOU WISH.
PHEW! MY, MY...
BRING ME BACK SOME YATSUHASHI TREATS.
THAT WAS EASY...

...
I DUNNO.
I GUESS I *DID* LEARN WHAT KIND OF YOKAI NURARIHYON ARE.
OH, YOU DID, HUH?
THEN...
YES.
I WILL BE LEAVING FOR KYOTO.

GWOoo
COME HERE.
WE MUST TALK.
SINCE YOU ARE BACK...
...I ASSUME YOU WERE ABLE TO GET OUT.
DID YOU LEARN ANYTHING?

YES.
HAVE MY ALLIES GET READY.
RATTLE
RIKUO ...
...YOU'RE BACK.
...
UH-HUH.

WHO'RE YOU?
I'M AMEZO THE NUMA-GAPPA.
HM?
ME? I'M A KAPPA TOO!
AHHH
I HAVEN'T THOUGHT OF A NAME YET.
WH-WHO ARE THESE GUYS?!
GRAH
HEY!! WHERE'RE YOU GOING?!
SWOOSH
GRAH
WHERE'D THEY COME FROM?! YIKES!
LORD RIKUO...?
W-WHAT IS GOING ON?
GRAH
GRAH
THEY'RE FROM TONO.
I'M GONNA SAY HI TO GRAMPS. KEEP THEM OUTTA TROUBLE.
THOSE ARE TONO YOKAI?
Trouble, indeed...
LORD RIKUO, ARE YOU GOING TO KYOTO?!
!

HEY! DON'T CLIMB THE SAKURA TREE!!
HMPH. SO THIS PLACE OVERSEES KANTO.
WHERE DO YOU TRAIN?
YAMMER
YAMMER
YAMMER
...
YOU'RE ...
... STINKY.
...
YOU SURE ARE A STRAIGHT-TALKER...
TMP TMP TMP
HOW ABOUT A TASTE OF HELL?!
KOFF KOFF
PEE-YEW!
WOO-HOO!
SPLASH
PTOOEY!
IT'S JUST A POND.
SPLOSH
SPLOSH
HRM?

ADUM
WELCOME BACK, LORD RIKUO!!
WHO ARE THESE PEOPLE?! YOKAI NOT FROM THE NURA CLAN ARE FORBIDDEN FROM ENTERING THE MAIN HOUSE!!
WHOA. THEY ADDRESS RIKUO AS LORD.
SPARE ME THE SERMONS, MONK.
BUT IF YOU HOLD OUT A BOWL ...
...I COULD GIVE YOU SOME ALMS.
HEY!!
ARE YOU MAKING FUN OF THE NURA CLAN'S STRIKE TEAM LEADER?!
HUNH?! I DON'T CARE WHO YOU ARE! I'M AWASHIMA THE AMANOJAKU!
IF YOU THINK I'M JUST A GIRL, YOU'LL REGRET IT!!
WHAT ?!
OH. I SEE. SORRY. YOU'RE A WOMAN?
THOK
RIGHT NOW I AM!! HANDS OFF, GROPER !!
WHAT'S THAT SUPPOSED TO MEAN?!

DA
ANYWAY...
...WE'VE ARRIVED AT THE NURA HOUSE!!
HEH HEH HEH...
DU
WE MADE IT!!
THERE A SWAMP HERE?
I'm thirsty...
RIKUO'S SO SLOW THAT NIGHT FELL BEFORE WE GOT HERE.
YAK
IT CAN'T BE HELPED! HE TURNS INTO A HUMAN DURING THE DAY!!
ITAKU, YOU TURN INTO A WEASEL, RIGHT?
YOU'RE BOTH SO CUTE!
YAK
WHO ARE THOSE GUYS?
YAK YAK
THEY'RE AWFULLY CASUAL WITH LORD RIKUO!

FWHAMM
M
YIKES!!
?!
EGAD! AN ENEMY ATTACK?!
GLANCE GLANCE
PUFF PUFF
HUH?!
IT'S LORD RIKUO!!
WHAT?!
YOU'RE RIGHT! LORD RIKUO...
...IS BAAACK!
HUBBUB
HMM...
THIS IS THE NURA CLAN?
WE FINALLY ARRIVED.
KOFF KOFF
ALL THAT RUNNING MADE ME SWEAT SO MUCH I ALMOST MELTED!
THIS PLACE IS PRETTY BIG.
RRMMMM

Act 77: Return Home

["Itachi" means weasel.]

DADUMMM

LET'S GO.
YAHOO! I CAN'T WAIT TO SEE KYOTO!
GOOD-BYE, TONO!!
HUH?! IS THIS YOUR FIRST TIME OUT OF THE VILLAGE, AMEZO?!
YEP!! I WONDER WHAT THE WORLD IS LIKE!

SHUF
HEY.
THAT SWORD... DON'T YOU EVER USE NENEKIRI-MARU?
That's just a stick (Takimaru) you picked up!
THE SWORD IS FOR FIGHTING BIGGER AYAKASHI...
...BUT THIS SIDEKICK IS ENOUGH FOR THIS VILLAGE'S FEAR.

SHING
I TOLD YOU NEVER TO DISSOLVE YOUR FEAR.
ITAKU ...
THIS HAS ALREADY KILLED YOU 200 TIMES HERE IN TONO.
YOU'RE NOT READY.
SWIP
SWIP
DADUM
AND I'M NOT DONE TEACHING YOU!!
BUT THAT DOESN'T MEAN I'M YOUR ALLY!!
...
THANK YOU.

YES!! PLEASE!!
HUH ?
SHUF
THE KYOTO AYAKASHI ARE REALLY STRONG.
SHUF SHUF
I NEED ALL THE HELP I CAN GET!!
SHUF
YOU GUYS CAN BE MY HUNDRED DEMONS!
SHUF
HEY NOW, RIKUO...
AT LEAST HE'S HONEST ...
WELL ?
WHADDAYA MEAN?
YOU PROMISED WE WOULD IF HE SAID THE MAGIC WORD!
I DIDN'T BRING MY MAKEUP ...
C'MON, GET READY AND LET'S GO!
HUH ?
NOW HE'S BOSSING US AROUND!
...
AREN'T YOU COMING, ITAKU?

NAMA-HAGE...
IF YOU WANT TO SAY THANK YOU, NOW'S THE TIME.
WE GOT SENT ON THIS ERRAND RIGHT AWAY.
OH...
THANKS FOR EVERYTHING.
RIKUO.
WE DON'T ALLY WITH ANYONE...
...BUT IF YOU SAY YOU NEED HELP AND ASK NICELY...
...WE'LL *THINK* ABOUT IT.

READ THIS WAY

...
RIKUO...
THEY ARE ALIKE.
YAMMER
HUH?
HE DISAPPEARED!
YAMMER
HE STROLLED IN...
...RAPIDLY GREW STRONGER...
WHAT JUST HAPPENED?!
YAMMER
...THEN TOOK SOME OF US WITH HIM WHEN HE LEFT.
I'M TAKING THESE GUYS.
YOU WANNA COME, AKA-GAPPA?
TAKE SOME OF US?
NO ONE FROM TONO WOULD GO WITH HIM!
IF I HAD NOT BEEN COMMANDER...
...I WOULD HAVE GONE.
WHAT?!

HRRM?
THANKS FOR EVERYTHING.
I'LL BE GOING NOW.
GLUP GLUP GLUP
YAMMER
L... LORD AKA-GAPPA...
H-HOW DID THAT HAPPEN?!
YAMMER

WHAAAT?!
WHAT DID YOU SAY?!
ARE YOU INSULTING TONO?!
YOU'VE GOT A BIG MOUTH, YOU!
YOU'LL NEVER LEAVE HERE ALIVE!!
GRAAAAH
?!

WHAT? DON'T YOU WANT TO SEE UP CLOSE...
...WHEN I BECOME LORD OF THE SPIRITS OF RIVERS AND MOUNTAINS?
...
WHAT DO YOU MEAN?
LORDING IT UP HERE IN THE MOUNTAINS...
...JUST MAKES YOU KINGS OF A BIG HILL.
I'M ASKING IF ANY OF YOU HAVE THE GUTS TO COME WITH ME TO KYOTO.

I AM GOING TO KYOTO TO MEET HER ONCE MORE...
...AND SEVER THE DEEP TIES THAT BIND US!!
HEY, NOW...
YOU'RE NOT GOING TO RESCUE SOME HOT CHICK?!
AW, MAN!
YAMMER
HAGOROMO-GITSUNE, LORD 400 YEARS AGO, WAS HIS FATHER'S ENEMY...
YAMMER
AND NOW THE YOUNG MASTER OF THE NURA CLAN WILL FIGHT IN PLACE OF THE AGING SUPREME COMMANDER TO BECOME MASTER OF THE AYAKASHI! COOL!!
NOW THAT'S SOMETHING TO SEE!!
AN EPIC BATTLE TO BECOME THE AYAKASHI MASTER!!
WE'LL BE WATCHING FROM HERE IN TONO!!
HA HA HA HA!

DID YOU NOT KNOW?
HEHHEHHEH
I BELIEVE I MET HAGOROMO-GITSUNE EIGHT YEARS AGO...
...WHEN MY FATHER WAS KILLED BEFORE MY VERY EYES.
?!
THE NURA CLAN WAS WEAKENING AND THE KANSAI YOKAI WERE BEGINNING TO EXTEND THEIR MIGHT.
THE SUPREME COMMANDER...?!
WHISPER
SO THE FOX HAS RETURNED...
WHISPER
I THINK THE ONE WHO KILLED MY FATHER IS HAGOROMO-GITSUNE.
THE YOUNG MASTER SAYS A YOUNG WOMAN WAS WITH HIM.
WHISPER

I WAS NOT HERE LONG, BUT EVERYONE IN TONO TOOK TIME TO TEACH A FLEDGLING LIKE ME.
YOU HAVE MY MOST HEARTFELT APPRECIATION.
OHH
YOU CAME TO OFFER YOUR RESPECTS.
DID YOU LEARN SUCH SOCIAL GRACE TO GAIN TONO'S FAVOR?
HA HA HA!
YOU HAVE BEEN LISTENING TO TALES OF YOUR GRANDFATHER.
SINCE LOSING THE PREVIOUS GENERATION, THE NURA CLAN HAS BEEN STEADILY WEAKENING.

!!
PARDON ME.
RIKUO ?!
FUMP
WHAT ?!
WHERE'D HE COME FROM ?!
HUBBUB
W-WHAT'RE YOU HANGING AROUND FOR, RIKUO?!
YAMMER
YOU SHOULD BE GONE BY NOW!
YAMMER
IT'S ALL RIGHT. PIPE DOWN.
I THOUGHT YOU WOULD LEAVE.
YOU'RE NOT DEAD, SO PERHAPS YOU ARE A LITTLE STRONGER NOW?
A LITTLE.

YAM MER
YAK YAK
YAMMER YAKYAK
GA HAHA
YAMMERYAMMER
CHATTER
...
KYOTO ...
KIDOMARU WAS INCREDIBLY STRONG ...
GUYS LIKE HIM ARE EVERYWHERE IN THE CAPITAL. HOW MANY IN THE NURA CLAN CAN STAND AGAINST THEM?

Act 76: Leaving Tono!!

HAGOROMO-GITSUNE!
FATHER!
WAIT!
HUFF HUFF
WELL DONE.
NOW OUR DREAM IS REBORN.
...
WHO ARE YOU, MISS?

HAGOROMO-GITSUNE ANNIHILATED THE ONMYOJI?!
I DON'T KNOW ALL THE DETAILS, BUT SHE BEAT ALL THOSE SKILLED ONMYOJI!
Act 76: Leaving Tono!!
RIKUO ...
YOU'VE GOT FRIENDS IN KYOTO, DON'T YOU?!
YOU SHOULD GO HELP THEM!!
YOU CAN CUT THROUGH THE VILLAGE'S FEAR NOW, CAN'T YOU?!

Q: DO YOKAI HAVE BLOOD TYPES? IF SO, WHAT TYPE IS KAPPA? (BY THE WAY, I'M TYPE B.)
-YOSSHI, GUNMA PREFECTURE

KAPPA: I DON'T KNOW MY BLOOD TYPE! MAYBE YOKAI DON'T HAVE BLOOD TYPES? EVERYBODY'S BLOOD IS A DIFFERENT COLOR, SO...

Q: RIKUO IS AN ONLY CHILD. YURA HAS AN OLDER BROTHER, BUT HOW ABOUT THE OTHER CHARACTERS? DO THEY HAVE BROTHERS AND SISTERS?
-KITTY, NAGANO PREFECTURE

KIYOTSUGU: I'M AN ONLY CHILD!! ALWAYS!!
MAKI: OKAY, FINE! AS FOR ME, I HAVE AN OLDER BROTHER IN HIGH SCHOOL. HE LIKES STREET RACING!

SHIMA: I'VE GOT LOTS OF LITTLE BROTHERS AND SISTERS.

Q: WHY DOES GOZUMARU CALL YUKI-ONNA LIL' YUKI?
-AME-ONNA, OKAYAMA PREFECTURE

GOZUMARU: HEY! THIS IS THE KIND OF QUESTION I GET? WHO CARES ABOUT THAT?

MEZUMARU: HOW ABOUT CALLING HER TSURARA? IT'S A CUTE NAME!

GOZUMARU: HUNH? WHAT ARE YOU? DUMB?

MEZUMARU: OUCH!! WHY YOU GOTTA GET ANGRY AT ME?!

Q: DO YOKAI CELEBRATE EVENTS LIKE NEW YEAR'S OR CHRISTMAS?
-RIO YAMADA, OSAKA PREFECTURE

KARASU-TENGU: YEAH! I CAN'T SAY THAT ALL YOKAI EVERYWHERE AROUND JAPAN DO, BUT THE NURA CLAN CELEBRATES EVERYTHING!! YOKAI BASICALLY ALWAYS ENJOY FUN STUFF. WE REALLY LOVE PARTIES. YOU KNOW THAT SONG? "JANUARY MEANS NEW YEAR'S, SO DRINK UP!" LIKE THAT. CHRISTMAS? WE LIKE WESTERN EVENTS TOO. ESPECIALLY HALLOWEEN!!

Q: THIS IS A QUESTION FOR RYOTA-NEKO! ARE YOU A CALICO CAT? OR IS THAT A BRUISE AROUND YOUR LEFT EYE?

RYOTA-NEKO: WH-WHOA! THAT QUESTION FOR ME CAME UP SO SUDDENLY I'M SHOCKED. I'M A CALICO YOKAI! MOST CALICOES ARE FEMALE. MALES ARE RARE. BUT I'M A MALE! MAYBE THAT'S WHY I'M A YOKAI!

Q: WHAT IS THE RELATIONSHIP BETWEEN KEJORO AND KUBINASHI?
-KURO-CHAN, IWATE PREFECTURE

KUBINASHI: WHAT KIND OF RELATIONSHIP? I GUESS WE'RE ACQUAINTANCES FROM WAY BACK.

KEJORO: DON'T ASK SUCH RUDE QUESTIONS!

KUBINASHI: HEY, WHERE'RE YOU GOING? UM...SORRY. IT LOOKS LIKE SHE'S IN A BAD MOOD. ASK AGAIN SOME OTHER TIME.

SOMEONE FROM TONO WHO'S IN KYOTO SENT A MESSAGE!
HAGOROMO-GITSUNE ANNIHILATED THE ONMYOJI!!
?!
KYOTO HAS FALLEN INTO HER HANDS!!

KSHA
NNG
HUFF
HUFF
HUFF
TOMP
...
THIS GUY'S FEAR IS INTERESTING.
IT'S MORE VERSATILE THAN I THOUGHT.
WHOOEE!
SMACK
RIKUO'S PRETTY TOUGH!
KLANG
UH-OH, RIKUOOO!!
AWASHIMA?!

THE NEXT DAY
WHAM
WHUD
TONO
HUFF
HUFF
GOOD. MAINTAIN YOUR INVOKE.
NEVER DISSOLVE IT DURING BATTLE.

KEIKAIN YASO-STYLE ONMYO JUTSU!
DEMONIC POSSESSION LANCE!
FOLLOW ME.
HERE I GO.

MY SPIRIT LANCE, KIOKU, IS UNDEFEATED...
EVEN WITHOUT THE SHIKIGAMI HAGUN, WE WILL NOT FAIL!!
POP
SNAP
AREN'T YOU...
...HUMAN?

URGH ...
WHOOSH
WHAT SHOULD WE DO, AKIFUSA?
GWOOOO
STAY CALM.
I WILL ATTACK.
YOU LEND SUPPORT.
RRMMM
AKI-FUSA ...
R-RIGHT...

YOU TOOK TOO LONG. NOW GASHA-DOKURO...
...HAS RIPPED THROUGH YOUR WALL OF GOLD.
RRMMM
HURRY UP AND SHOW ME...
...WHAT YOU MEANT BY "STRONGEST."
...

SNAP
KRACK
RRRIP

BOOM
UGHAH!

?!
WHAT'S THAT?!
WAIT. THIS IS JUST GETTING GOOD...
KRIK KRAK
KRAK
...GASHA-DOKURO.
SNAP SHRRED
OHHH! ♡ THERE YOU ARE...
RRIP KRACK
...LADY HAGOROMO-GITSUNEEE! ♡

GA
BOOM
LADY HAGOROMO-GITSUNEEE!
WHERE ARE YOUUU ?!
PRESS
ARE YOU HERE?
I WILL HELP YOUUU!
PRESSS

OH...
...I WOULD LIKE TO SEE THOSE THINGS.
WHAT?!
I MEAN ...
...ARE THEY PRETTIER THAN THIS WALL OF GOLD?
SWUF
FIRST SHOW ME THAT KEKKAI BARRIER AND SHIKIGAMI.
I CAN'T WAIT.
SWUF
SWUF
SWUF

SH
AND THEN THERE'S THE STRONGEST SPIRIT BLADE- YASO STYLE! SPIRIT LANCE!! KIOKU!!!
WITH THESE, WE WILL DESTROY YOU!!
ING
IN THE SKILL OF MAKING SPIRIT BLADES...
...I AM PROUD TO HAVE SURPASSED THE 13TH HEIR!

FOUR HUNDRED YEARS AGO, WE OF THE KEIKAIN FAMILY SEALED YOU AWAY...
...BY USING THE SHIKIGAMI HAGUN AND THE SPIRIT BLADE NENEKIRIMARU!!
NO ONE HERE CAN USE HAGUN...
TUMP
...BUT AFTER 400 YEARS OF STUDY, WE CAN DO MUCH MORE!!
MASATSUGU KEIKAIN OF THE FUKUJU FAMILY ISOLATED YOU WITH THE STRONGEST KEKKAI BARRIER...
SWIP
IT'S MY FIRST TIME TO SEE...
...A NINE-TAILED FOX YOKAI.
...AND PATO KEIKAIN OF THE AIKA FAMILY...
...IMMOBILIZED YOU WITH THE STRONGEST SHIKIGAMI.
YOU GO, GOMORA-MARU!!
HA HA!

HA HA!
DON'T LET HER ESCAPE...
...MY DEAR SHIKIGAMI! ♡
WHORLMMMM
...
RRM
MM
MASTER OF AYAKASHI ...
...YOU MAY NOT ADVANCE ANY FURTHER.
CLOMP

HWIP
HWIP

SMUS
SHHH
YOU DID IT!!
SMASHED HER FLAT!!

GO...
...MY DEAR SHIKIGAMI GOMORA-MARU!!
ZASLOSSH
HEY...
...NOW I CAN'T SEE.

THATH
OOM
CRACKLE
CRACKLE
FUKUJU-STYLE BARRIER JUTSU! PANORAMIC WALL OF GOLD!
YOU CAN'T GET OUT AND NO ONE CAN GET IN.
AH, HOW BEAUTIFUL!
IT REACHES THE SKY!

Act 75: Rokukinji Temple Battle

Act 75: Rokukinji Temple Battle

NURA: RISE OF THE YOKAI CLAN

SWUF
I SEE. A GOLDEN TOMB. HOW STYLISH.
BUT YOU ONMYOJI ARE THE ONES GOING INTO IT!!
SWUF
SWUF
SWUF

YOU CANNOT LEAVE AND NO ONE WILL COME TO HELP.
WE HAVE THROWN UP A KEKKAI BARRIER TO CONTAIN YOU.
TONIGHT, IN THIS PLACE...
...YOU WILL RETURN TO DARKNESS, YOU OLD FOX!!

GYAAH!
OWWW!
W-WHAT'S THAT?!
AGH!
RRMM
LADY HAGOROMO-GITSUNE?!
DHOOM
FLUP
FLUP
HAGOROMO-GITSUNE...
...WE HAVE ISOLATED YOU.
PLIP
PLIP

AFFS
SSHH

GWOOM
OOH! SHINY GOLD!
I HAVEN'T SEEN THAT FOR 400 YEARS...
DOESN'T IT LOOK NEWER NOW?
LADY HAGOROMO-GITSUNE, IT'S SHINING!!
THE CAPITAL REALLY DOES HAVE THE BEST STUFF!!
FWOOO
NOW I KNOW WHY YOU WANT THIS PLACE!
IF IT WEREN'T FOR THE PEOPLE, THE CAPITAL WOULD BE BEAUTIFUL!
THAT'S RIGHT. HEH HEH...
ALL RIGHT, SHOW ME A FLASHY SIDESHOW AS BEFITS THIS TEMPLE.

THE NEXT SEAL IS ROKUKINJI TEMPLE.
WE WILL STRIKE THEM THERE.
THIRD SEAL.
ROKUKINJI TEMPLE.

READ THIS WAY

FIRST SEAL
YASO FAMILY: AKIFUSA KEIKAIN
...BUT THE CAPITAL.

READ THIS WAY

THEN WE SHOULD REMOVE THE CURSE BY KILLING THE FOX.
SECOND SEAL
AIKA FAMILY: PATO KEIKAIN

THIS ISN'T A CONSTRUCTIVE CONVERSATION.
THE PROBLEM IS WHEN AND HOW WE CAPTURE HAGOROMO-GITSUNE.
SSSIP
N... NO, MASA-TSUGU.
DO YOU KNOW HOW HARD IT IS TO RAISE A SINGLE ONMYOJI?
INDEED...
MUR MUR
...GITSUNE HAS CURSED THE KEIKAIN FAMILY BLOODLINE.
Keikain Clan Main Family Tree
Hidemoto
THE MEN OF THE MAIN FAMILY PASS AWAY EARLY.
THAT IS WHY THE BRANCHES HAVE ALWAYS PROVIDED TALENTED INDIVIDUALS FOR THE MAIN FAMILY TO RAISE.
THE BLOODLINE MUST NOT END!!

THIRD SEAL
FUKUJU FAMILY: MASATSUGU KEIKAIN
WE DIDN'T COME HERE TO DECIDE WHO GETS KILLED NEXT.

READ THIS WAY

RRR
HAGOROMO-GITSUNE IS MERCILESS.
MMMM
FUSHIME INARI, HASHIRA VILLA, RYUENJI TEMPLE, SEIEIJI TEMPLE, NISHIHOUGANJI TEMPLE...
8
5
6
7
4
IN JUST 13 DAYS, SHE HAS DESTROYED FIVE SEALS.
CHATTER
CHATTER
THERE ARE ONLY THREE LEFT.
ONLY THE GUARDIANS OF THE FUKUJU FAMILY, AIKA FAMILY AND YASO FAMILY REMAIN.
W-WHAT CAN WE DO?! WE MUST REINFORCE THE THIRD SEAL!!
WE HAVE NO CHOICE!!

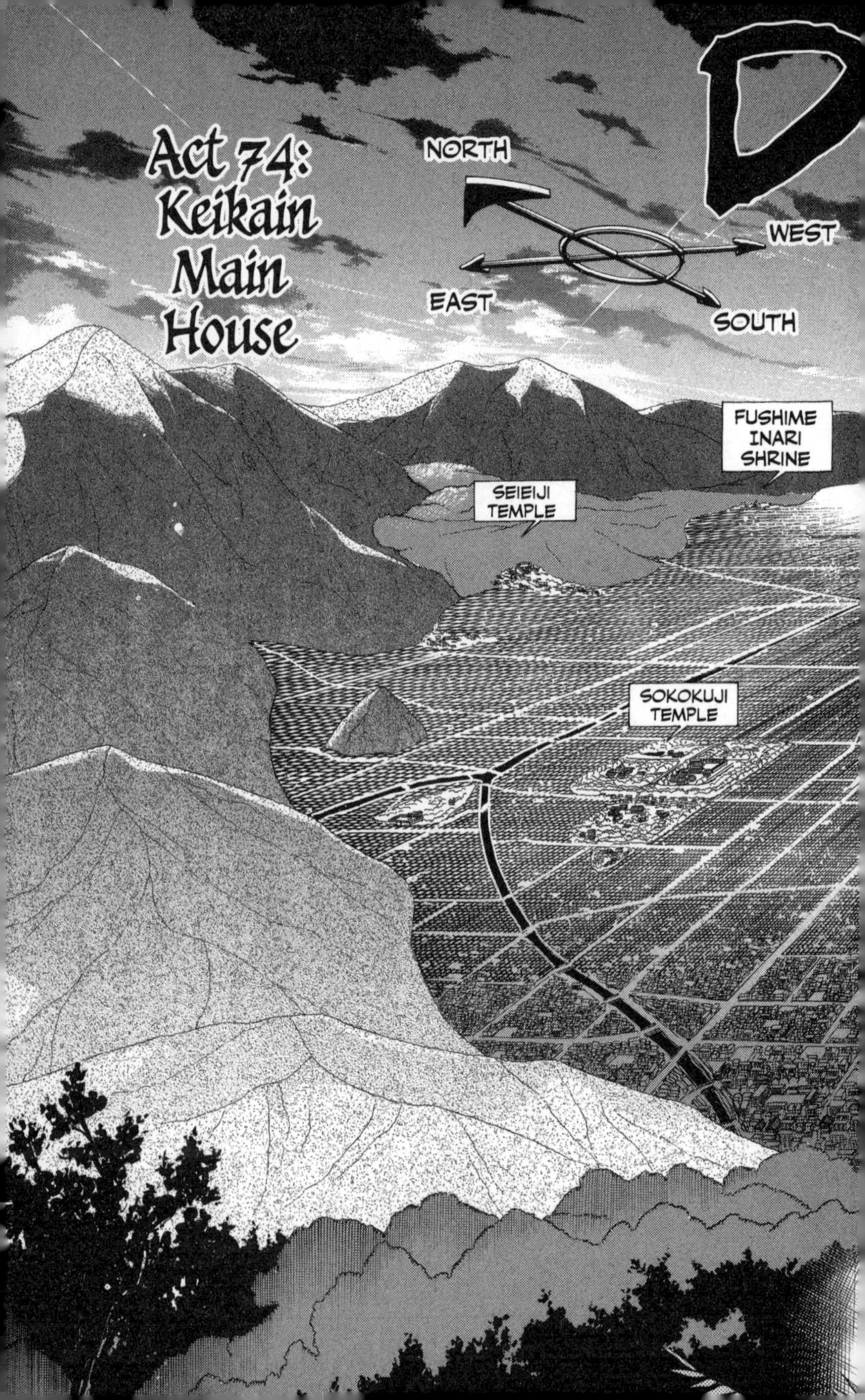
D
Act 74:
Keikain
Main
House
NORTH
WEST
EAST
SOUTH
FUSHIME
INARI
SHRINE
SEIEIJI
TEMPLE
SOKOKUJI
TEMPLE

ADOOOM
HASHIRA VILLA
NISHIHOUGANJI TEMPLE
NIJO CASTLE
RYUENJI TEMPLE
ROKUKINJI TEMPLE

GADADOOOM
HEH HEH HEH!
HEE HEE HEE!
THOOM
THEY BROKE THE SEAL AT NISHIHOUGANJI TEMPLE.
THE YOKAI ARE ADVANCING DIRECTLY INTO RAKUCHU.
YURA... MAMIRU...
IT'S ALMOST TIME.

WHOA !!
WHAT'S THAT?!
?!
GASHA-DOKURO ?
IS THIS WHERE YOU'VE BEEN?
I GOT SEALED IN. IT'S BEEN A WHILE, LADY HAGOROMO-GITSUNE.
I HAVE BEEN WAITING FOR THIS DAY.
KATHOOM

Three days after the fall...
...of Seieiji Temple.
OH!
THERE IT IS!
RRRMMM
Act 74: Keikain Main House
The fourth seal.
Nishi-hou-ganji Temple.
TWITCH TWITCH
KOFF KOFF
GAGK!
RRMMM
PLEASE REMOVE THE SEAL, LADY HAGOROMO-GITSUNE.
RRMMM
AN AYAKASHI CANNOT TOUCH IT WITH BARE HANDS.
WHUNK

NURA: RISE OF THE YOKAI CLAN

...N...
OOPS.
SWUF
SWUF
I ACCIDENTALLY KILLED HIM.
SWUF

BEHOLD!! KEIKAIN CLAN IDORO-STYLE ONMYO JUTSU! YANG POWER ENHANCEMENT PILLS!!
BWA HAH HAH HAH! BY THIS, THE STRONGEST ONMYO JUTSU, I INGEST THE POWER OF YANG DIRECTLY INTO MY BODY!!
NO ONE CAN STOP ME WHEN I'M LIKE THIS, YOU VIXEEEEEEEE—

GAWHOOM
SO WHO'S GONNA KILL HIM?
MAKE THIS SIDESHOW ENTERTAINING.
I'LL DO IT!
HEH HEH!
HE'S JUST A MIDDLE-AGED WEAKLING!
GYAH HA HA!
MWA HAHA
HM?
I'VE BEEN WAITING, YOU MONSTERS...
GAFFSSHH

HAVE CONFIDENCE, HAIGO KEIKAIN!!
YOU HAVE THE FRUITS OF YOUR RESEARCH!!
B-BUT IF I DRINK THIS...
DO IT!! IT IS A REFLECTION OF YOUR TALENT!!
NO... IT IS TOO DANGER-OUS...
HUFF
HUFF
HUFF
FOOL!! IF YOU DIE, THAT'S THE END!! DRINK IT!!
UNNNGH ...
UNNNNNNGH !!
DA DOOM
DA
THERE HE IS!
THE FOURTH ONMYOJI!

SEIEIJI TEMPLE IS SURE TO BE NEXT!!
THERE'S NO MISTAKE! ACCORDING TO THE PATH OF THE SEALS ESTABLISHED BY THE 13TH HEIR...
...I'M THE NEXT TO DIE!
I WANTED TO BE FAMILY HEAD! THAT'S WHY I STUDIED SO HARD!!
TOK TOK
NEXT THING I KNOW, I'M 43!!
My nickname is Vice-principal...
I KNOW BECAUSE OF MY RESEARCH! I WAS BORN IN THE WRONG ERA!! THE SEALS ARE WEAKENING!
WAAH! I DON'T WANNA DIEEE! I WANNA BE FAMILY HEAD!
YOU CAN DO IT.
YOU ARE MORE THAN CAPABLE OF HANDLING THIS.

FIFTH SEAL
SEIEIJI TEMPLE
UNGH...
TRMBL TRMBL
UNGH...
UNGH...
TRMBL
WHAT'S WRONG WITH THAT GUY?
I DON'T KNOW. HE KEEPS SHAKING. SCARY...
UH-OH!! THERE ISN'T ANYONE AROUND!!
HUUUH?! TEMPLES CLOSE SO EARLY...
UNNGH... UNGH...
FUSHIME INARI... HASHIRA VILLA... RYUENJI TEMPLE...

Act 73:

Hagoromo-Gitsune's Kyoto Invasion

WE WILL TRANSFORM THIS WORLD INTO A BLACK PARADISE.

HEE HEE HEE...
...I THOUGHT YOU WOULD SAY SOMETHING LIKE THAT, LADY HAGOROMO-GITSUNE.
RRMMMM
LET ME HANDLE TONIGHT'S WORK...
NO, I'LL DO IT!
I'M YOUR NUMBER ONE MINION!!
HEH HEH... I LEAVE IT IN YOUR HANDS. DO AS YOU LIKE.
ALL RIGHT, LET US BE GOING.

...WHEN IT IS OVER, WE WILL BUILD A CASTLE...
...UPON NIJO CASTLE, LOCATION OF THE FIRST SEAL.
AROUND NEW NIJO CASTLE...
...WE WILL FILL RAKUCHU WITH AYAKASHI.
LADY HA-GOROMO-GITSUNE ...

C'MON, DO WE REALLY...
...HAVE TO FOLLOW THE ROUTE THEY DECIDED?!
HEH
INTEREST-ING.
ONE BY ONE, AS IF TRACING A SPIRAL.
AYAKASHI ADVANCING INTO RAKUCHU. IT THRILLS ME SIMPLY TO IMAGINE IT.
LADY HAGOROMO-GITSUNE...
...THIS IS A WAR OF TOTAL EXTERMIN-ATION WITH THE ONMYOJI.
FOR ME IT IS A MERE SIDESHOW, BUT...

THE ROADS OF THE CAPITAL CONNECT THESE EIGHT TEMPLES, SHRINES AND CASTLES...
...IN THE FORM OF A SPIRAL!!
THE SPIRAL IS THE SAME SHAPE AS THE SEAL THAT THE GREAT MONK TENKAI ESTABLISHED WHEN CONSTRUCTING EDO CASTLE.
THAT SPIRAL PRESERVED PEACE IN THE EDO SHOGUNATE FOR 300 YEARS.
THE CAPITAL HAS LASTED FOR 400 YEARS.
THE POWER OF GENIUS ONMYOJI HIDEMOTO THE 13TH HEIR HAS SURPASSED GREAT MONK TENKAI'S BY 100 YEARS!!
A STRONG SEAL PROTECTS EACH OF THE EIGHT LOCATIONS.
WE MUST TRACE THE SPIRAL AND ERADICATE THEM ONE BY ONE.

VIP
VIP
MINAGOROSHI-JIZO, ARE YOU CHICKEN? LET ME DO IT!!
SHALL I CURSE THEM TO DEATH—STARTING WITH YOU?
VIP
VIP
VIP
FUSHIME INARI SHRINE.
HASHIRA VILLA.
RYUENJI TEMPLE.
SEIEIJI TEMPLE.
NISHIHOU-GANJI TEMPLE.
ROKU-KINJI TEMPLE.
SO-KOKUJI TEMPLE.
NIJO CASTLE.

VIP
FOR 400 YEARS WE HAVE DRUNK THE BITTER CUP.
THE ONMYOJI SEALED US AWAY.
VIP
MMM
RRRR
I UNDER-STAND HOW YOU FEEL..
...BUT YOU MUST NOT TAKE OUR OPPONENTS LIGHTLY.
WE CANNOT DESTROY THEM ALL AT ONCE BECAUSE OF THE POWER OF HIDEMOTO, THE 13TH HEIR.
IN THE KEICHO PERIOD, HE ESTABLISHED THE SPIRAL SEAL FOR REPELLING EVIL.

WHY DON'T WE JUST ASSAULT THEM ALL AT ONCE?
THIS IS IRRITATING ME...
...MINA-GOROSHI-JIZO.
VIP
YEAH. LET'S TAKE BACK THE CAPITAL AS SOON AS POSSIBLE.
THAT IS OUR DEVOUT WISH!!
RRMMM
INDEED...
HEEHEE HEE...
VRRR
THAT'S RIGHT...
I'M ITCHIN' TO GO...
VIPVIP

CLINK
CLINK
LADY HAGOROMO-GITSUNE...
YES, I SEE... DRY AND RARE... OTHERWISE, THE HUMAN LIVER WOULD LOSE ITS POWER...
WELL...
...TODAY WE UNDO THE FIFTH SEAL.
Hee hee hee...
VIP
ABOUT THOSE SEALS ...

CREAK
CREAK
OH...
MISTRESS...
HAVE YOU PREPARED DINNER AS I REQUESTED?
CREAK
CREAK
Y-YES, MISTRESS. IT IS READY.
GOOD. AS USUAL, DO NOT ALLOW ANYONE TO ENTER.
Y-YES, MISTRESS.

Act 73
Hagoromo-Gitsune's Kyoto Invasion
I WILL WAIT BELOW WITH EVERYONE ELSE.
Hee hee hee...
CHAK

NURA: RISE OF THE YOKAI CLAN

I AM AWAKE, MINA-GOROSHI-JIZO.

IN LESS THAN TWO WEEKS...
RRRMMMM
...THE CAPITAL AND THE ONMYOJI WILL FALL INTO LADY HAGOROMO-GITSUNE'S HANDS.
Heh heh heh... LADY HAGOROMO-GITSUNE...
...IT IS TIME TO WAKE UP.
TODAY...
...WE UNDO THE FIFTH SEAL.
Heh heh heh...
...
LADY HAGOROMO-GITSUNE?

RRMMM
I DO NOT INTEND...
...TO ANNIHILATE TONO...
...BUT I WILL REMEMBER THAT YOU HELPED THE GRANDSON OF NURARIHYON.
I WILL KILL EVERYONE—LIKE THE KEIKAIN—WHO COOPERATES WITH THE NURA CLAN.

MISTER, YOU CAN'T ESCAPE THAT PRISON OF ICE.
UNLESS YOU WANT TO FREEZE TO DEATH...
...SAY YOU'RE SORRY AT THE TOP OF YOUR VOICE...
...FOR BEING UNRULY IN OUR VILLAGE.
TOK
TOK
YOU...
ITAKU!! THESE ARE KYOTO YOKAI!!
EXPLAIN WHAT'S GOING ON!
TUMP
TUMP

TATA
KRAK
WHAT? ICE?!
KRIK
KRAK
KRAK
KRAK
I NOTICED YOU WERE LATE.
TOK
ITAKU, YOU'RE IN CHARGE OF TEACHING RIKUO, AREN'T YOU?
SO DON'T DO ANYTHING DUMB.

NOW IS MY CHANCE...
...TO CRUSH HIM!!

NURARIHYON YOKAI...
...SHIFT AWARENESS AND CUT THROUGH FEAR!!
HMPH.
SNAP
IT'S BROKEN. GUESS YOU CAN'T DEFEAT YOKAI WITH A WOODEN CLUB.
FLUMP
UGH
UGH
DON'T DISSOLVE YOUR FEAR, RIKUO!

IT DISAPPEARED!
HA HA HA! OF COURSE!
RIPPLES BREAK MEIKYOSHISUI THE WAY THEY DISRUPT A MIRROR-LIKE SURFACE OF WATER.
KYOKA-SUIGETSU DISAPPEARS—LIKE THE MOON REFLECTED IN THE WATER.
IT... SLIPS AWAY.
JUST LIKE WE NURARI-HYON.
GWOooo
KYO-KA-SUI-GETSU.
I SENSE HIM, BUT HE ISN'T THERE!!
HRMPH!
ONE STYLE OF CLASSICAL CHINESE IS CALLED THE KYOKASUIGETSU METHOD.
IT AVOIDS CLEAR EXPLANATION IN FAVOR OF VAGUE SUGGESTIONS CALLING FORTH CONTENT FROM WITHIN THE READER'S HEART...
...INCREASING THE PRESENCE OF WHAT ISN'T THERE.
THIS IS AN UN-EXPECTED AND DANGEROUS FEAR!

HE WAS TRYING TO SOUND COOL AND SAID...
...THAT NURARIHYON ARE "A FLOWER REFLECTED IN A MIRROR, A MOON FLOATING IN WATER."
IN OTHER WORDS, KYOKA-SUIGETSU.
AN AYAKASHI THAT EMBODIES DREAMS.
LOOK, GRAMPS!
THE MOON IS OUT EVEN THOUGH IT'S DAYTIME!
YOU'RE RIGHT. THAT'S STRANGE.
BUT LOOK AT THE POND, RIKUO. YOU CAN SEE THE MOON'S REFLECTION, SO IT ISN'T AN ILLUSION.
YEAH! THE MOON'S IN THE POND!
SPLOSH
HUH ...?!

KRAKKK
!!
KRIK
THE VILLAGE'S...
HE CUT THROUGH THE VILLAGE'S FEAR!!
GRAMPS ONCE TOLD ME LONG AGO...
...WHAT KIND OF YOKAI A NURARIHYON IS.
SHMP
KRIK KRIK

WHAMM
KRASSHH
URGH ...
FWUP
THE AFTER-SHOCK FROM THE IMPACT ...!!

SWISSH
I COULDN'T FEEL HIM AT ALL!
...?!
SWIP
!
WHAT'S GOING ON? I CAN SENSE HIM, BUT...
SPIN
Y-YEAH!! YOU'RE RIGHT!!
I CAN'T TOUCH HIM!!
BUT HE'S RIGHT THERE!!
WHAT'S THE DEAL?!
UH-OH.
HE'S GOT US!

SWOO...
HUUUNH ?!
WHAT DID YOU JUST DO?!
SHOOM
MORON! I'LL KILL HIM!

?!
...
SWOOO
HUNH ...?!

SUFFER MY POSSESS!
SPINNING BULL FORCE!!
SNAPPOPBULGE
GRAAAAH

RRRMMM
CLOMP
CLOMP
THIS GUY...
NO, WAIT. THIS GUY'S FEAR...
RRMMM
OH, RIGHT.
RIKUO'S INVOKE WAS BECOMING UNDETECT-ABLE.
THEN THIS ISN'T...
...INVOKE!!
WHAT ARE YOU?!
I THOUGHT I CUT THROUGH YOUR FEAR!!
GRAAAH

Act 72
Kyoka-
suigetsu
Tono
Monogatari,
Part
4

CLOMP
CLOMP
Act 72:
Kyokasuigetsu Tono Monogatari, Part 4
GASP
CLOMP
CLOMP
WHAT ?!
THAT'S A COMPLETELY DIFFERENT FEAR THAN BEFORE!!

NURA: RISE OF THE YOKAI CLAN

RRUNK
GRB
SKRR
I JUST REMEMBERED ...
KYOKA-SUIGETSU.
SHTUMP

GRRR
WHO'RE YOU?
YOU WANT ME TO DEVOUR YOU, IDIOT?
STRING HIM UP. IT'S SETTLED.
FATUMP
WAIT...
...ITAKU.
HE'S...
...MY ENEMY.

FWUD
D
...?!
AGH...
?!
VEEN
WHAT'S GOING ON HERE?
TOMP
DO YOU KNOW WHAT I DO TO KYOTO YOKAI...
HEY...
...WHO RUN AMOK IN OUR VILLAGE?
I KILL THEM.

REMEMBER!
YOU SAW IT ONCE!
WHOOM
?!
THAT'S IT!

FACE YOUR BLOOD AS THE YOKAI CALLED NURARIHYON.
THEN YOUR TECHNIQUE WILL BECOME CLEAR.
TADUM
CHOMP
THAT'S RIGHT, RIKUO!
IT'S THAT AMANO-JAKU...
BING
AT FIRST, I COULDN'T STAND MY CHARACTER-ISTICS!
BUT NOW I CHANNEL IT INTO A SPECIAL TECHNIQUE!!
...?
YEAH, AND AN AMAZING TECHNIQUE IT IS. TEE HEE...
ONLY YOU CAN DO IT. I CERTAINLY CAN'T!
YOU WANT ME TO DO IT RIGHT NOW, ITAKU?!
...
CHANNEL-ING INTO THE NEXT STEP...
WHAT DID GRAMPS DO THAT TIME?

...ARE YOKAI WHO SNEAK INTO PEOPLE'S HOUSES AND DRINK THEIR TEA. THEY'RE THE SUPREME COMMANDER OF ALL YOKAI.
NURARIHYON ...
...
THAT'S HARD TO UNDERSTAND.
KOFF KOFF
YOU'RE NOT VERY CONCRETE.
Stop messing around.
THAT'S NOT MY FAULT!
I'm not messing around!
HE'S RIGHT.
I UNDERSTAND MEIKYOSHISUI, BUT BECOMING UNDETECTABLE IS...
YOKAI-WISE IT'S...
THAT'S WHY YOU CAN'T GET A FEELING FOR THIS.
WHY NOT START BY GETTING TO KNOW YOURSELF?
Here! Lemon slices and honey!

EVERYONE HAS...
...A DIFFERENT FEAR.
USING FEAR AS AN ATTACK...
...MEANS MANIFESTING YOUR CHARACTER-ISTICS AS A YOKAI IN A PHYSICAL WAY.
WHAK
WHUD
A KAPPA'S ATTACK INVOLVES WATER.
A YUKI-ONNA'S ATTACK MANIFESTS IN ICE.
SPRAAY
what a ridiculous attack!
OHHH, I SEE.
AND A KAMAITACHI ATTACKS WITH A SICKLE.
THAT'S EASY ENOUGH...
WHAT KIND OF YOKAI IS A NURARIHYON?
BAM
POW
SPRAAAY
TOMP

BUT OUR DREAM IS REBORN.
CLOMP
WE WILL CLAIM THE CAPITAL AND SEVER THE NURA CLAN'S LIFE THREAD!!
SW
I WILL SEND YOUR SEVERED HEAD...
OOM
...TO LADY HAGOROMO-GITSUNE AS A SOUVENIR.
AND I'LL SEND YOUR TRUNK TO YOUR GRANDFATHER WITH A DECLARATION OF WAR IN FOX SCRIPT.
THIS OLD DUDE'S NUTS!
TRMB
TRMB
HE'S GONNA KILL ME!
WHAMM
THAT'S NO GOOD AT ALL.

GWOOOM
THE CHILD HE HAD WITH THAT NOBLE-WOMAN?
NO, YOU DON'T SEEM 400 YEARS OLD.
OH, I SEE. THE GRANDSON.
YOU'RE ABOUT THAT AGE.
THAT WAS WHEN...
...TIME STOPPED FOR THE KYOTO YOKAI.

Kidomar the Kyot Yokai, Tono Monogatari, Part 3

YOU'RE NOT HIM.
I AM KIDOMARU.
WHO ARE YOU?

...
NO, WAIT.
THAT MAN'S FEAR WOULDN'T BREAK SO EASILY.

URNGH!

THEY DIDN'T HESITATE TO ATTACK.
THEY CAN'T SEE ME, BUT I'M UN-ARMED.
RIGHT NOW...
...ALL I CAN DO IS RUN!!
TOK
STOMP
HMPH!

UNH? HE DISAP-PEAR-ED!
WSHWSH
HE FALL BETWEEN THE ROCKS?
CLOMP
DON'T LET HIM FOOL YOU.
HMM. I WAS RIGHT. IT IS HIM.
USING FEAR TO DISAPPEAR... THAT IS THE FEAR THAT NURARIHYON USED TO STRIKE LADY HAGOROMO-GITSUNE...
TUMP
TUMP
WHOA! HE ALMOST KILLED ME!
WHO ARE THOSE GUYS?!

FOOM
DRRRMMMMM
...!!
KR/K KR/K
...
FOOOMP

THOOOM
CHAAAH!
...
WH...
WHOA !!

Act 71: Kidomaru, The Kyoto Yokai Tono Monogatari, Part 3
KRIK
KRAK
KRIK
?!

Rikuo's bed in Tono.

I CAN'T EVER FORGET THAT FACE!
CLOMP CLOMP
MY WORST MEMORY.

HM?
WAIT.
IT'S JUST A LITTLE BRAT.
LOOK OVER THERE.
NO, THAT'S ...
THAT FACE ...
FLUMP
WHEW. THAT SHOULD DO IT FOR A WHILE.

YOU DISPATCHED FIGHTERS TO THAT ACCURSED NURA CLAN BEHIND OUR BACKS.
WE WILL CRUSH THEM WHEN WE CRUSH THE NURA CLAN.
IF YOU CAN, THEN DO IT.
WE ARE NEUTRAL. BUT IF YOU INSIST ON PICKING A FIGHT...
...YOU WILL FALL ONCE AGAIN.
HEH HEH HEH
WHAT DID YOU SAY?!
CHAK
ENOUGH.
I WILL REMEMBER YOUR WORDS. AND WE WILL BE BACK.
I AWAIT YOUR REPLY.
I HOPE YOU MAKE IT OUT SAFELY.
THAT OLD FOOL...
SHALL WE KILL TWO OR THREE VILLAGERS AND STRING THEM UP AS A LESSON?
THAT WOULD ONLY HAVE THE OPPOSITE EFFECT ON THEM.

IT PAINS ME THAT I CANNOT WELCOME YOU...
...LORD KIDOMARU.
SPARE ME THE INCONSIDER-ATE CHATTER, LORD AKAGAPPA.
AS YOU KNOW, LADY HAGOROMO-GITSUNE HAS RETURNED.
IN ONE TO TWO WEEKS, SHE WILL OPEN THOSE HATEFUL SEALS IN THE CAPITAL.
I NEED 20 TO 30 OF YOUR BEST FIGHTERS RIGHT AWAY.
IMPOSSIBLE.
OUR OBLIGATION TO KYOTO DOES NOT EXTEND THAT FAR.
THEN YOUR TIES TO THE NURA CLAN ARE MOST *UN-FORTUNATE*.

MORNING HAS DAWNED.
Kyoto Yokai Kidomaru
RRR
MMMMM

YOU CERTAINLY DO COME HERE FROM THE CAPITAL OFTEN.

FOOSH
SHRIP
RMM

THEY THINK I'M JUST A WOMAN!
HUH?
A-AWASHIMA?!
HUH?! AWASHIMA THE AMANOJAKU?!
WASN'T HE A GUY?!
GASPLASH
I'M A YOKAI THAT'S A BOY BY DAY...
...AND A GIRL AT NIGHT!!!
WE'LL GET ALONG REAL NICE, NEW BOY!!
WE CAN EVEN SEE EACH OTHER NAKED!
NOW CUT THAT OUT!
RRRK
SMI
UH... HEH HEH HEE HEE...
STOP STARING, AMEZO!
...

AS THE KINGPIN OF THE MILITANT FACTIONS THROUGHOUT TOHOKU, THE TONO FAMILY HAS SENT FIGHTERS TO ALL THE YOKAI ORGANIZATIONS AROUND THE COUNTRY.
WE DON'T FOLLOW ANYONE AND WE DON'T ALLY WITH ANYONE. WE REMAIN SELF-RELIANT.
THAT IS OUR PRIDE AS THE YOKAI NINJA OF TONO.
OTHERS LOOK DOWN ON US, BUT THEN USE US WHEN IT SUITS THEM!!
YEAH, THEY'RE REAL SNOBS.
THAT'S RIGHT! THEY SNUB US, THEN REQUEST SOLDIERS!!
BUT WE DON'T WORK FOR THEM!!
KAPASSH
NEXT TIME THEY SHOW UP, WE'LL KILL 'EM!
SPLOSH
SLURSH
NO MATTER WHAT THE OLD GUYS SAY!
YEAH!! I HATE THOSE KYOTO GUYS!!
TOK

SHE RISKED HER LIFE TO PROTECT ME.
I CAN'T JUST ABANDON HER.
I DO HAVE ANOTHER REASON, THOUGH.
Just "all right"?
I bet she's a knockout! I can tell...
THE YOKAI CODE.
OHH! LIKE YOKAI YAKUZA!
HUH?
ITAKU...
SO KYOTO'S YOUR ENEMY.
I DON'T...
...LIKE THOSE GUYS EITHER.
OUR LAND IS A SUPER COLD AND UNBOUNTIFUL ONE.
THROUGHOUT HISTORY, WE HAVE SUFFERED DEFEAT BY THE CENTRAL LANDS.
THAT IS WHY THIS LAND'S AYAKASHI HAVE GROWN STRONG.
SO WE CAN SURVIVE ON OUR OWN!!

IT ISN'T THAT EASY, IS IT?!
Shut up!
IT ISN'T? I DID IT WHEN I WAS 5.
A YOKAI JUST NATURALLY DOES IT.
OH...
RIKUO, WHY ARE YOU SO OBSESSED WITH KYOTO?
HM?
WE'VE BEEN HEARING STRANGE RUMORS ABOUT KYOTO.
SOMETHING ABOUT A TROUBLE-MAKER COMING BACK. IS IT DANGEROUS?
YEAH.
I GUESS SO. I MEAN, YURA...
YURA? A CHICK?!
YOU GONNA SAVE HER? SHE MUST BE PRETTY!
SPLOSH
WELL, SHE'S ALL RIGHT.

SO THIS IS WHAT'S AT THE TOP?
I THOUGHT I SAW A BIG POT, AND IT'S AN OUTDOOR BATH!
PHEW
AHHH
HIS WOUNDS MUST STING.
HEH HEH HEH
RIKUO COULDN'T DO IT EVEN ONCE TODAY.
MAYBE HE ISN'T CUT OUT FOR IT.

THAT WOULD BE NO DIFFERENT THAN DYING WHILE I'M WEAK.
I'LL LEARN IT EVEN IF IT KILLS ME—AND THEN GO TO KYOTO!
KYOTO?
HEH...
EVERYONE HERE LOVES TO FIGHT.
ALL WE DO IS SPAR!!
SMILE
ALL RIGHT!! I'LL SHOW YOU MY FEAR!
I LIKE YOUR SPIRIT!! HERE I COME!
I'M NEXT!
GLOMP
HUH?
JUST WAIT A—
HUH? ONE AFTER THE OTHER?!
WAIT! I'M WOUND-ED!
OW!
YAMMER YAMMER
OH...
...AND DON'T FORGET TO DO THE LAUNDRY AND PREPARE THE BATH!

SO THAT'S WHAT GRAMPS WAS DOING...
AN AYAKASHI'S NEXT STEP...
I WON'T BE ABLE TO BEAT THE KYOTO YOKAI WITHOUT IT.
PLEASE.
TEACH THAT TO ME!!
YOU MUST BE READY TO DIE IF NECESSARY ...
...OR I WON'T WASTE MY TIME.

CUTTING THROUGH FEAR... YOU MIGHT ALSO CALL IT BREAKING FEAR.
KCH
TO DO SO, YOU MUST CHANNEL FEAR, WHICH BEGINS AS NO MORE THAN A THREATENING PRESENCE, INTO A PHYSICAL ATTACK.
BREAK FEAR WITH FEAR. THIS ANTI-AYAKASHI COMBAT TECHNIQUE...
FEAR
FEAR
FEAR
FEAR
FEAR
...WAS A NECESSITY IN YOKAI HISTORY.
FEAR
FEAR
FEAR
HERE IN THIS VILLAGE...
...WE CALL IT *POSSESS.*
DA
DUM

SLASH
SLASH
OOPS ...
THRUNK
HEE HEE HEE! YOU OVERDID IT, ITAKU!
GAFFS
YOU TRYIN' TO WRECK THE SPARRING GROUND AGAIN?
!! I SAW HIM!!
KOFF KOFF
ITAKU CUT THROUGH HIS FEAR!!
UNGH ...

SHUNK
RMMM
YOKAI NINJA ART! WIND KNIFE!
THAT'S MY SECRET TECHNIQUE.

THE TRANSFER OF INVOKE...
... POSSESS!
VRMMMM
RMMMM
!!
WHAT? HE CONCENTRATED FEAR...
...IN HIS SICKLES !!
GRAAAAAH!

THE BRINGING OF FEAR...
...INVOKE...

READ THIS WAY

HUH ?
HE DIS-APPEARED!
IS THAT A NURARI-HYON'S FEAR?!
RAAHHH
NO WAY! HE DID IT TO EVERYONE HERE?!
CLOMP
STAY BACK !!
I'M FIGHTING HIM!
I'M THE ONE WHO'S GOING TO...
...CUT THROUGH HIS FEAR.
TOK
TOK
...

LIKE THIS...?
!!

UH-OH...
ALL RIGHT, BRING IT ON.
I FELT SORRY FOR HIM IN PAJAMAS, SO I LENT HIM CLOTHES.
YAMMER YAMMER
They look good!
I HEAR HE BEAT SOME GUYS IN SHIKOKU.
SHIKOKU? WEREN'T THEY CRUSHED A LONG TIME AGO?
...
LET'S SEE... HOW DO I DO THIS AGAIN?
RIKUO, STILL YOUR HEART.
I CALL THIS MEIKYOSHISUI.
URGH
GRAMPS!

HEATING THE BATH IS WORSE.
I'M IN CHARGE OF CLEANING AND LAUNDRY.
I'M REIRA, THE YUKI-ONNA. AND THIS IS YUKARI, THE ZASHIKIWARASHI. YOU'RE IN THE NURA CLAN?
YOU'RE NURARIHYON'S GRANDSON?! I'M DOHIKO, THE FUTTACHI.
PLEASED TO MEET YOU.
WELL MET!
HE DOESN'T EVEN KNOW ABOUT FEAR.
SERI-OUSLY?!
BUT HE'S THE NURA CLAN'S YOUNG MASTER!
THAT'S INCON-CEIVABLE FOR A YOKAI!
PAMPERED BOY...
WOAH
I CAN TOO BRING FEAR!
OH, YOU CAN, HUH?
THEN SHOW US.
...
ARGH!

THUMP
A NEW FACE!
OH, HIM? ITAKU HAS TO TEACH HIM.
IDIOT! DON'T SAY THAT!
I'M AMEZO, THE NUMA-GAPPA.
YOU GONNA CLEAN THE BATHTUB FOR ME?
Hee hee hee...
AND CHOP WOOD. THAT'S THE HARDEST CHORE AROUND HERE.
I'M AWASHIMA, THE AMANOJAKU.

THEY INSTILL FEAR, AWE AND RESPECT.
THE TERM FEAR SUMMARIZES ALL THOSE YOKAI POWERS.
A YOKAI BRINGS FEAR WHEN HE AMPLIFIES HIS PRESENCE TO SURPRISE AND OVERWHELM.
※Bringing Fear!
IT INVOLVES CONTROLLING THE ATMOSPHERE.
YOU KNOW, LIKE IN SPOOKY STORIES.
A CHILL CREEPS INTO THE AIR...
...AND THEN A YOKAI CAN USE HIS ABILITIES.
BUT THAT ONLY WORKS ON HUMANS.
AS TIME PASSED, YOKAI INCREASED IN NUMBER AND BEGAN FIGHTING OVER TERRITORY.
A WAY TO FIGHT AYAKASHI BECAME NECESSARY.
THAT IS CALLED THE NEXT STEP.
...
HM? WHO'S THAT, ITAKU?
TUMP TUMP
GOOD TIMING. GATHER EVERYONE TOGETHER.

BOOM
WHOA!!
YEEEK
SKIDD
HA HA HA!
TAKE IT EASY, MAN!
THAT'S FEAR.
SEEING IT IN ACTION BEATS ANY EXPLANATION.
YOKAI EXIST TO SCARE PEOPLE, RIGHT?

WHACK
WHAM
WHUD
BAM
WHOK
...
THEY'RE NOT REALLY GETTING INTO IT. THEY MUST JUST BE WARMING UP.
NOT GETTING INTO IT?
THEY'RE TOTALLY HAMMERING EACH OTHER!
NOW THEY'RE GETTING SERIOUS.
LOOK. AMEZO THE KAPPA IS GOING TO BRING FEAR.

WHAT IS THIS PLACE?
THE LARGEST OF TONO'S MANY SPARRING GROUNDS.
SPARRING GROUNDS?
THEY'RE WHAT'S SPECIAL ABOUT TONO.
A KAPPA AND AMANOJAKU ARE FIGHTING.
LET'S WATCH.

TUMP
WHSH
HEY!
WAIT! KAMAITACHI!
JUST DO THE LAUNDRY!
I'VE GOT LESSONS!
TELL ME ABOUT CUTTING THROUGH FEAR!
WHSH
...
RUSTLE
!

Illustration of Kappabuchi, Tono

Act 70: Kamaitachi Tono Monogatari, Part 2

TABLE OF CONTENTS

NURA: RISE OF THE YOKAI CLAN

9

NATSUMI TORII

A member of the Kiyojuji Paranormal Patrol, but like Maki, she has no particular interest in yokai. At one point, a yokai curse put her on the brink of death.

SAORI MAKI

Although she participates in the Kiyojuji Paranormal Patrol, she has no particular interest in yokai. She has a well-proportioned body for a middle school girl.

HAGOROMO-GITSUNE

A great Kyoto yokai who has a fateful connection to Nurarihyon and the Keikain family. She possesses humans and forces them to do evil things. She was revived after 400 years.

ITAKU

A yokai who lives in the Tohoku region's Tono Village where Rikuo is sent. He kept an eye on Rikuo, who was trying to escape from the village.

KUBINASHI

ZEN

MOKUGYO-DARUMA

KARASU-TENGU

STORY SO FAR

Rikuo Nura appears to be just your average seventh-grader at Ukiyoe Middle School. But he's actually the grandson of the yokai Overlord Nurarihyon and has just been promoted to become the Underboss of the Nura clan, the Tokyo region's powerful yokai syndicate! For now, he lives his days as a human boy, but eventually, he is expected to take his grandfather's place as the leader of the clan.

A long time ago, a human woman named Princess Yo was abducted by underlings of Hagoromo-Gitsune, a powerful yokai intent on stealing her internal organs in order to find out the source of Princess Yo's great power. Rikuo's grandfather, Nurarihyon, helped by Hidemoto, the 13th Keikain Style Master, saves Princess Yo and the two are wed.

Back in the present day, Hidemoto's barriers, which have held Hagoromo-Gitsune back for 400 years, are being broken. Rikuo wants to go to Kyoto to help his friend Yura, who is on the front lines of the fight. But Nurarihyon instead sends Rikuo to the Tohoku region's yokai village of Tono to train.

CHARACTERS

NURARIHYON

Rikuo's grandfather and the Lord of Pandemonium. He intends to pass leadership of the Nura clan—leaders of the yokai world—to Rikuo. He's mischievous and likes to dine and ditch.

RIKUO NURA

Though he appears to be a human boy, he's actually the grandson of Nurarihyon, a yokai. His grandfather's blood makes him one-quarter yokai, and he transforms into a yokai at times.

KIYOTSUGU

Rikuo's classmate. He has adored yokai ever since Rikuo saved him in his yokai form, leading him to form the Kiyojuji Paranormal Patrol.

KANA IENAGA

Rikuo's classmate and a childhood friend. Even though she hates scary things, she's a member of the Kiyojuji Paranormal Patrol for some reason.

YUKI-ONNA

A yokai of the Nura clan who is in charge of looking after Rikuo. She disguises herself as a human and attends the same school as Rikuo to protect him from danger. When in human form, she goes by the name Tsurara Oikawa.

YURA KEIKAIN

Rikuo's classmate and a descendant of the Keikain family of onmyoji. She transferred into Ukiyoe Middle School to do field training in yokai exorcism. She has the power to control her shikigami and uses them to destroy yokai.

NURA: RISE OF THE YOKAI CLAN

9

TONO MONOGATARI

STORY AND ART BY
HIROSHI SHIIBASHI

NURA: RISE OF THE YOKAI CLAN

NURA: RISE OF THE YOKAI CLAN
VOLUME 9
SHONEN JUMP Manga Edition

Story and Art by HIROSHI SHIIBASHI

Translation – John Werry
Touch-up Art and Lettering – Annaliese Christman
Graphics and Cover Design – Fawn Lau
Editor – Joel Enos

Printed in the U.S.A.

Published by VIZ Media, LLC
P.O. Box 77010
San Francisco, CA 94107

10 9 8 7 6 5 4 3 2 1
First printing, June 2012

2010 is the 100th anniversary of the birth of *Tono Monogatari* written by Kunio Yanagida. When I drew the Tono story arc in 2009, I thought, "Too bad this isn't coming out next year, the timing could've been perfect!" But fortunately, it turned out that the tanko is coming out 2010 (LOL). So, I now present the *Nura: Rise of the Yokai Clan* version of *Tono Monogatari*!!

—HIROSHI SHIIBASHI, 2010

HIROSHI SHIIBASHI debuted in BUSINESS JUMP magazine with *Aratama*. NURA: RISE OF THE YOKAI CLAN is his breakout hit. He was an assistant to manga artist Hirohiko Araki, the creator of *Jojo's Bizarre Adventure*. *Steel Ball Run* by Araki is one of his favorite manga.